The Ordinary Sublime

ANHINGA PRESS

The Ordinary Sublime

POEMS

PATRICIA WATERS

ANHINGA PRESS, 2006
TALLAHASSEE, FLORIDA

Cover art: C.L. Knight, *Digital painting and collage*
            using family photo from Patricia Waters
Author photo: Jan Burleson of Burleson-Brown Photography
Cover design, book design, and production: C. L. Knight
Typesetting: Jill Ihasz
Type Styles: titles set in Tiffany; text set in Bernhard Modern

Library of Congress Cataloging-in-Publication Data
The Ordinary Sublime by Patricia Waters – First Edition
ISBN – 0-938078-94-1 (978-0-938078-94-4)
Library of Congress Cataloging Card Number – 2006929378

Generous support from the Ayn Foundation
permitted the publication of this work.

This publication is sponsored in part by a grant
from the Florida Department of State,
Division of Cultural Affairs, and the Florida Arts Council.

Anhinga Press Inc. is a nonprofit corporation dedicated wholly
to the publication and appreciation of fine poetry and other literary genres.

For personal orders, catalogs, and information write to:
Anhinga Press
P.O. Box 10595
Tallahassee, Florida 32302
Web site: www.anhinga.org
E-mail: info@anhinga.org

Published in the United States
by Anhinga Press
Tallahassee, Florida
First Edition, 2006

To my sons,
Forrest and Marcus,
to whom I owe so very much,
and to the memory of my parents.

CONTENTS

ENDINGS

ACKNOWLEDGMENTS

My thanks to the editors of the following publications where some of the poems in this book appeared:

Appalachian Life: "Carny"

Arts and Letters (forthcoming): "Morning Coffee," and "Where Does Terror Come From"

Birmingham Poetry Review: "O Prince," "Why I Live in the South," "A Word from Heaney's Translation of *Beowulf,*" and "The Warren Cup"

Chattahoochee Review: "A Key to Endings"

Iron Horse Review: "On a Frosty Morn"

Knoxville Writers Guild anthology: "*Erro, Errare* Means I Wander, To Wander"

Louisville Review: "The Ordinary Sublime," and "As Heard Early Morning on National Public Radio, September 16, 1996 While Driving from Athens to Knoxville"

POMPA (Publications of the Mississippi Philological Association): "El Sueno de la Vida," "Spring, Untitled," "Work, for the Night is Coming," "The Dress," "Out of These Things," "What's Left When It Won't Go Away," "How I Turned Up Dead in the Grocery Store Parking Lot," "Yeah, Sure," "Proverbs," and "After Reading *Kremlin of Smoke*"

Southern Humanities Review: "Giving Suck," and "The Stone Breakers"

"Now is the Drinking," and "Rose," a section of "Attar," were published in Cy Twombly artist catalogues by Gagosian Gallery.

The generosity and support of so many people made the publication of these poems possible. However I must single out for particular gratitude two whose confidence in the work, whose imaginative worlds brought me so very much — Heiner Friedrich and Cy Twombly.

I wish to thank Dean Barbara Dewey and the Libraries of the University of Tennessee for the residency and support that permitted the gathering of these poems into manuscript form.

And last but not least, I wish to thank the Ayn Foundation for the generous support that permitted the publication of this work.

THE ORDINARY SUBLIME

DAILY LIFE

PROVERBS

I could have stayed home
living like Proverbs,
price above rubies — and all that,
clean kitchen, scrubbed heart.

Dining room chairs do not match,
doors lock at night
on a mind that failed,
minotaur become labyrinth.

Get out say the curtains,
fly into hot sun,
fall into blue sea,
drown in such a bold story.

GIVING SUCK

The hunger,
the bawling, furious demand:
food now, not later,
Now the bald open mouth squalls
and in answer the breasts, heavy,
become heavier and fill,
fill so full
they begin to leak,
twin spots of damp on the shirt,
there is the fumble
with buttons, with hooks,
one hand, the other
holds the hungry,
eyes closed tight with fury,
but the blind nose
already smells milk
so the mouth starts to mew
and search, fists flailing
hit at last the naked flesh
and open, fingers splay
in pleasure
as the mouth opens
and closes hard and sure
on the tit, now overflowing,
the milk spurting and gushing
into the sudden quiet,
the mouth filling, so much milk
it runs out the corners,
down the cheeks
into the neck's fat creases.
There is the swallowing.
When the mouth lets go,
the head pulls back, then lolls,
mouth wet, open,

lips a little blistered,
an arm dangles,

a hand lies flat against the breast
as for one instant
eyes meet
in silence, in satiation,
a shared glance that closes
into the sleep of life.

FOR YOU

The hour is late. All is still.
I am working on the words
I want to pack with those Sunday afternoons
when, in the car with your parents,
father driving, mother still wearing her hat,
happiness opens before you — the blackberries you find
by chance, the road shadowed by great trees
undulant with the wind, birds scattering,
surely, you think, with joy
because they fly, because they sing.
You lie in greenest grass, watching clouds —
the sun warms you. In light-filled air you dream
to the sound of voices. When you wake,
someone is there, saying you are home.

STUNG

In the first chill mornings of October
I watch and wait for the yellow jackets
to emerge, later each day, more slowed,
less angry, so I might lug the box away
from the back door. The box's heap
of old maps — AAA, National Geographic —
are now compounded with their saliva
and cellulose into their nest, from which
they have taken insult at my presence,
stinging me on three occasions.

The worst, about the ankle, laid me up
in high summer, ankle elevated,
its angry red swelling tight and hot,
under ice pack — three days
of cautionary drugs, of magazines.

This morning, the coolest yet,
while coffee jets through the expresso
machine, I pull the box from its perch
onto the driveway and though I expect
a reaction, am still surprised by their surprise,
how quickly they fly out their matted gray cave.
They are really pissed now.

Through the window I can see my coffee
steaming into the cup
but I cannot get to the door,
some engine of memory
is driving the swarm back
to the blank space
where the box had been.

I want my coffee — grab the bomb
and spray. Their bodies drop.
The air is suddenly quiet,
the smell is funky,
I go inside to wash my hands.
When I bring the coffee to my mouth,
my hand has a chemical smell, like shame.

ON A FROSTY MORN

It is bigamy both to love and to dream.
— Odysseus Elytis

The dog frisks, all nose and joy,
as we cross fields to where
white rimes the broomy, sedgey stuff
around cedars, regal in their deep green tang.
Day breaks with memory:
my father, his old army jacket,
pockets bulging with shells,
shotgun over his arm,
is calling the dogs, Buck and Queen.
He always uses the same names,
no matter what generation of dog.
He has his own economy.

Now I walk this season,
cold air sharp in the lungs,
not hunting for birds.
This time of day, this time of year,
I hear his voice,
the sound of blood, of place
where I knew what things were.

My breath returns in clouds.
I cross dead fields.
Mist drifts in strands over black water,
bare hardwoods lace their brachiated bodies
for restless birds; their sudden songs
open the day down here, even in winter.
Before you know it, twilight is come,
dull fat pink sun going fast,
short steps down to the end of something.

In my dreams I meet them face to face.
I forget the questions I have always wanted to ask,
can only wonder how love survives the grave,
how they are there, handfast and smiling,
how I sleep in that presence, a place
            wordless, understood.

SPRING FIRST DAY

Under the bird song
the pulsing alarm
no one turns off,
pear blossoms stink,
embarrassment of the crotch,
heated by this first day of spring.
War somewhere, forsythia rampant,
a small carpet of violets waits
for the two-stroke engine,
free market sentiment,
trees are still tight with bud,
gauzy green,
we are born to death, desire
is what the world says,
the feral black cat comes to food,
roiling the dirt to relieve
its urgent estrus,
and everywhere birds, throats open
in lyric purpose, not noise,
never random,
cry their deep song — spring, life,
no more postponements,
the fountain of tears renewing itself,
the bicycle propped against a brick wall,
Mother, where are you buried?
Once I was my body.

SPRING, UNTITLED

1   How it bursts, first green from bare bark,
spring with its dying eyes,
the mother you will never see again,
the other's return, inevitable surprise.
Crocus persists, hyacinth shelters under
bridal wreath. Forsythia streams in the wind.

2   Searching the streets of Paris for one face,
you disappear in your desires.
Lenten Paris is cold; you hunch your shoulder
against rain and dread, take a chance on Notre Dame,
its heavy door shuts on the world.

In that created space, hovering over the devout,
the lookers-on, a vast and dusty dim.
Along the nave, the altar
large enough for any sacrifice,
wavering gold tears of massed candles,
blaze of white vestments.
In its dark stalls the choir shimmers,
one voice let loose upon the air.
What song conjures the bread,
the strong wine of ancient arbors,
those days of rejoicing
what the earth yields, how we endure?

3   Day breaks you again and again,
What do you hoard from foreign cities,
those strangers and their stories?
What darkness covers you,
what space do you carve with your longing?

In your bed, under the trees that witnessed your birth,
and will outlive you, you ponder the feral breath of night.
Under their sway, in deep and moonless dark, you sleep.
In the quick and agile fetching that is summer,
that is your dream, you are entire.

APRIL

There comes a time in the afternoon,
a moment when one realizes
the day has become inevitable.
No more opportunities,
only the swift onward pitch
into twilight, into dark.
At this moment I feel like I am falling —
afternoon at its most balmy,
when bees fumble at the azalea like inept lovers,
when the air is a mist of dogwood,
gauzy pink, green, and white,
when the birds have attained their manic calm,
a cool underbreath of breeze lifts the shade,
lets it fall, the sun warm yet remote,
the sky crystalline with promise, more light, more light —
that moment, then, has its most particular desperation.
What hour of light am I?
What approaches ahead of its own cry?

SEPTEMBER, DONE

Under the blue we lay
in green idleness,
cloud pursuing cloud
down the hours.
Summer never failed us.

Those carnal anarchs, magnolias
in moonlight, their bridal breath,
lure me to night ride in bicycle quiet
past ghosts living in the blue light
of their screens.

No matter how dark,
I find your room,
whatever I touch,
I steal. Roses fling
their scent over white fences,
down long porches.

I am rocking into this,
you becoming shade,
even as we look.

HOUSEWIFE

What we did was wrong.
It ended terribly,
how could it not?
There were children, houses,
whole rooms of the past
with no connecting doors.
We were night, whispers,
fugitive kisses, two beds,
yearning years, diapers, colic,
the marriage a dead land
hammered by drought.
The storm when it comes
is furious. Then everyone is hungry.

I cook, clean, sew, mend,
my heart like that Christmas present
bought at the July sales, packed away
somewhere, I find by accident,
long after the holidays are over.

THE LAST YEAR I WAS MARRIED

It has just gone winter,
we are in the new house,
my perfect kitchen,
the beautiful views.
I want a fire, bring in wood,
seasoned oak, and kindling.
It lights with no trouble,
I sit before the hearth,
twilight becoming solid dark,
and watch the fire bloom.

There, in the grate,
something begins to wake
from its winter sleep
and moves in the heat,
folding over itself,
in curl after curl.

I grab a poker, move to get it out,
realize the snake is on fire,
that I do not want to touch it.

I watch it burn to its quick end
on the hot wood, twisting,
writhing into black ash.
The next morning I find
the faint oily mark
it left on the new hearth.

For all I know,
it may still be there,
that serpent smear.

ERRO, ERRARE MEANS
I WANDER, TO WANDER

There is no arriving,
only going
till a stop,
empty tank,
empty stomach,
full bladder,
tired body,
a stop all too brief
till the getting up,
filmy matter in the eyes,
half-remembered dreams,
shower, coffee, then the road again,
day's going, a careful watching.
There is the conversation with the radio,
news of financial markets,
disappearing species of flowering plants,
never-ending tournaments,
ludic emptiness,
and music of such beauty
that you must stop and weep
because you do remember
what came before the road
when you were still yourself.

LA VIE QUOTIDIENNE

Daily life:
hear how English
sinks the words?

Dirty wash water,
last night's dinner dishes,
empties, piles of paper,
unmade bed.

~

This loneness,
my children now walk
their heads touching heaven.

Money, the years.

I'm tired, she said,
too many crows these days.
They eat the scraps
put out for the birds
that sing.

~

The drying rack blew over,
fouling clean laundry,
breaking the sunflower,
young green stalk.

Housework: futile, absurd.
Flower defeats me.

~

June promises,
July threatens,
August all elegy,
first leaf turning.

The logistics of cooking for twenty —
no more difficult than for two or for one.
One: a tray, television,
lost conversations in the head,
vodka goes with anything.

TORN PAPER

Here on this hill
this place of stones,
so young,
grass green my heart.
Shade overtakes me
or is it shadow
I confuse with her,
that woman
I have become —
she burns.
I know I die.

Sun, stone, silence —
this path up the mountain,
vineyards noon still,
walls hot, lizards crackle,
updraft from the sea,
zest of air, lemon trees
fat yellow lozenges in deep green —
my bride clothes are stored
in another country,
first infidelity
always the sweetest,
so alive, so dying —
I hate him.
I remember his mouth.

CHARTING

If I sail to your island,
carrying the world's wealth in my pockets,
will you still discover me?
For my glass beads, my calico, my steel knife,
my charts, my transit of Venus, will you
let me lie in the Oceania of your embrace?

From the Pacific of our imaginings,
Captain Cook brings back the word *taboo*
to new mouths, to different rooms.
Is taboo the thing forbidden
or the act of forbidding?
Is it that I cannot look
or what I cannot look upon?
Si fas est, if it is unspeakable,
as the Romans say,
is it the sea that I desire
or the sweetness of drowning there?

EL SUEÑO DE LA VIDA

We shore and we are the stuff of shores,
a littoral life, this picnic, this afternoon.

Here you lie in the umbrella's shade,
the book in your hands, your eyes on the sea.

In your pocket is the last letter
addressed to your thirst, to your hunger.

Drink, it is love in this cup.
Eat, the salt in the bread, only tears.

AFTER READING *KREMLIN OF SMOKE*

a poem by Gjertrude Schnackenberg

It is not that I cannot imagine this —
this imaginary interior life of Chopin,
intensely rendered. It is sustaining the act,
having to carry the scenario over —
études, as I pour drano into
scummy backed up bathwater,
nocturnes, as I check my e-mail,
preludes, as I pay bills, make a grocery list,
that first recording bought
in the Memphis State bookstore,
basement of the student center,
black vinyl Vox, dollar ninety-eight,
I played and played and played,
Ingrid Haebler, I have her still,
a second disc found at a going out
of business sale as I had worn out the first,
waltzes I played over and over —
as I had worn out so much else, my youth,
my capacity to forgive, but never,
never to wear out these turns, counter-turns —
his music an embrace, coupled arms, guiding,
sustaining, whirling circle true,
always completing itself, to the measure, just.

HOUSEWORK

I am in the kitchen unloading the dishwasher,
not because I want to,
but I am boiling two eggs for lunch and toasting toast,
black raspberry jam to the ready,
so might as well do something productive,
and I am thinking about how my mama had to light
a fire under me for me to do anything around the house,
nose always in a book — exasperation in her voice.
But I heard the pride in it. After all, who helped her pronounce
all those hard words in the Bible, Melchizidek
just tripped off my tongue, so I kept on reading and now
I look with Mother's eyes at the mess in my house
so bad I'll have to give a party,
and I wonder what difference does it make
whether my house is clean,
is neat, is neither, sure, I take out the trash,
wash me, the linens, the dishes —
but dust? I'd just be moving it from one place to another,
comes back like a bad memory, credit card debt rolling over.
Sometimes I am curious about the tipping point,
what will push me over the edge — to mop the kitchen floor,
scrub the bathtub, vacuum the carpet.
Why do I feel no urgency about this?
I shout up to heaven, to Mama —
you didn't fail. I know what I am supposed to do.
Hands push and shove words around
from one place to another, nose in a book.

THE ORDINARY SUBLIME

— for Sis

Tonight at 11 o'clock
I stand in my kitchen
peeling new potatoes
that I've just boiled
and shall have for supper
tomorrow. Something
in that calm repetitive action
goes for nothing
and for everything,
another day, another meal,
same as life, might be life.

MADE THINGS

NOW IS THE DRINKING

Nunc est bibendum

When the gods leave
do you think they hesitate,
turn and make a farewell sign,
some gesture of regret?

When they leave,
music is loudest,
sun high, stores fat
with harvest

and you, dizzy with wine,
befuddled with well-being,
sink into your body
as though it were real,
as if yours to keep.

You neither see their going
nor hear their silence,
you sleep,
bereft of dreams
in your good bed.

THE TOMATO IS NATIVE TO THIS PLACE

I am eating a tomato sandwich
and looking at a picture
of Vermeer's *Little Street* in a magazine,
the usual Vermeer words come to mind: stillness,
silence, quietude. There is a kind of thrum —
loud, unmoving silence found in rooms
where someone eats and reads alone.
Vermeer has turned his pocket of quiet inside out:
this is a street scene, big with builded lives, cellars of food,
capital for long winters. There is an all embracing sky,
as countries with low horizons have.
The blue is rain clean,
clouds gone hunting for distant gods.
Human figures are small,
faces bent to their daily repetitions,
mending, cleaning, economy of the house.
I want to step into that country with its patient earth,
burghers gambling in tulips,
interest accumulating like spices in the warehouse,
Middle Passage an ocean away,
someone else's latitudes, another word for *light* there.

THE STONE BREAKERS

Metamorphic, igneous, sedimentary,
the samples for first-year geology,
collected in that little box, with its partitions
to keep the specimens in their places,
the rock's name in black ink
on small white squares glued under it:
obsidian, mica, granite, limestone, pyrite,
fool's gold. More fool I for having forgot
so much, for having failed to learn
the facts of the world,
obdurate, as Dr. Johnson's stone,
I kick it thus, he said, a small gesture
when compared to the breakers of stone,
their backs bent to their labor,
Courbet, John Brett, painting stone,
the things of the world,
seeming permanence of matter,
stone the most fixed of fixed things
yet no more stable, no more still than light.
Millais' portrait of Ruskin
his good hard head, his iron soul,
he stands between Scots stone
rising beside him, the swift running burn
at his feet, highland water, its downward course
all mutability and Millais making love to Effie
in the afternoons because she has pubic hair,
because Ruskin daren't look at dimpled,
palpate, pocked, imperfect flesh
so far from the ecstasy he knew at Lucca,
Carrara's white imaginings,
blue veins of perfect marble breasts,
the tight, closed crease, stone smooth
where her legs fork.

BACCHUS AND ARIADNE

Titian calls it *poesie*,
I call it heartbreak.

She pushes outward
shoving the horizon,
Theseus,
that ship,
farther.

She has sheathed her big body
in precious ultramarine;
a long cloth,
the red tongue of desire,
is wrapped round her
twice.

He, the god, is followed
by that little wine-soaked crowd,
all appetite and noise.
He, the god,
white flame of his body,
flings fate upon her,
the net of stars,
as their eyes meet.

HOPPER'S *ELEVEN A.M.*

That peculiar strong American light —
Get going, it says, *sell something* —
makes a failure of the life that sits
in a chair before an open window
naked but for her shoes.
She watches that muscular
didactic light. We look at those shoes,
the road always implicit in America.

THE *EIDOLON*

The room at the back
of my mind
where nobody lives
but lots of stuff
stored for whatever
rainy day, bits about
Lewis & Clark,
Bonnard's self-portraits,
restaurants in New Orleans,
movies by the reel,
that free-standing room of vases
in the British Museum,
the little ones with narrow necks
holding perfumed oil for the dead,
newly so. Grief sharp, eyes
raw with tears, the mourning ones
not yet giving up the idea —
not really gone, just away somewhere,
sitting in an old shed
by the sea, the one window
high in the wall, open,
so you cannot see it but yes,
can hear it, can hear the sea
swallow your name.

THE WARREN CUP

Room 70, Case 12, British Museum

My hands smell of the parsley I headed
before heat hit the garden. Dream residue
weights a morning already heavy with wet.
More rain promises the blank white sky —

was it that story by William Gay,
a stew of jealousy, love, and infidelity,
her shooting him, that I read before bed?
Or the break-up down the street?
Yesterday I borrowed Billy's lawnmower,
not a mention of Jeffrey's name, ten years,
then nothing. Why did I wake
thinking of the Warren Cup?

Silver, hammered over 2,000 years ago,
it sits in a glass case atop a column.
How its two scenes surprised me,
man and younger lover, youth and boy —
erastes and *eromenos*,
the technical terms meaningless now
yet somehow leading, the two pair engaged,
a mutual concentration. Where do their eyes look?

Not at the middle-aged woman who looks at them,
with envy or with what? Compassion? Sadness? Regret
for having learned the declension, from desire to yearning,
to memory of yearning? There is the obedient servant
looking round the door of that room
where the black wine of Eros is poured out.

I wonder who looks at me while I stop here,
so move on, walking downstairs past the great stone slabs,

where the winged bull commanded by Sennacherib for his palace
lies on its side, being drawn on a sledge by enslaved myriads,
forever about to arrive at the gates of Nineveh — Sennacherib,
not yet murdered by his sons, Nineveh, not yet dust.

ABSTRACT

In the purity of the color
a space opens
for the gods to enter.

Motherwell's white,
the white of Argos,
the setting out.

Rothko's empurpled black,
dark sail,
omen,
fate.

.

LITTLE GOLDEN BOOKS
OF CHILDHOOD

LITTLE GOLDEN BOOKS OF CHILDHOOD

1

There are no crumbs left to scatter.
What impels you to follow that path?

There, a clearing, the cottage
you know from your dreams.

Smoke coils the chimney.
Rocking by the fire,
the crone of memory waits,
your name, the taste in her mouth.

2

In my village there is no nostalgia,
no road to that place
with long golden afternoons,
the tavern with little tables
under awnings, the linden alley — pears
ripening against lichened stone walls,
that path by the river, take my dress off once,
everyone knows, sweetest raspberry jam,
color of your lower lip when you bite.

3

Let down your hair,
let down your hair,
I missed the call,
too busy listening
to candles burning,
the narcissus,
winter's white stars,

descend from scent to stink,
what a common story,
door shut fast,
tower sealed with paper,
the furious mice,
eating those words.

4

Summer is the tower,
she lets down her hair, sweet slur
of scissors against silk,
lush leaves push against screens,
birds jostle in leaf shadow,
their constant chatter,
warm air on skin, afternoon dreams,
cool baths, scented soaps, clean linen
days going room to room,
book to book, hours of insistent,
silent conversation, the letters,
do they arrive?
In the mirrors this solitude,
silver and joy glint
like river water,
like something she runs after,
and cannot catch, laughing.

5

O Prince
I have call waiting.
My hair is growing,
the tower heated, no thorns,
all roses, as for that dragon,

a sweetheart
when he gets to know you,
dark forest of whispers,
of lost children, ringed
with sprawl. O Prince,
I am waiting,
times are changing,
calendars accrue, baskets
of old datebooks, phone numbers
where strangers answer, address
unknown, no forwarding —
do not delay, my Prince,
do not tarry, I am besieged
by what devours love,
what is more.

6

It is the dream,
the one that wakes you
though you are still asleep
yet you know
you are dreaming that crone
deep in the tangled wood,
wind streaming
through bare branches heaving,
you are looking into
the crackling snap of flame,
you are heat and chill,
if she speaks, it will come true.

7

Spell

It is like driving with your father at dusk,
you are in the front seat,
your feet not touching the floor,
but dangling
like the rest of your life
and the radio is tuned to nobody's news
when the voice becomes *once upon a time,*
there were living in a cottage in a wood,
and the car is suspended in time, in place,
tendrils, thick and green, twine round the car,
a great verdant hush you, your father drive into,
and the kingdom is ruled wisely, justly
until the jealous one, the fairy witch
of great power takes offense at such happiness and ...

8

What are the words
that whisper us what we know?
What did that spinner tell us?
The one unheard, then silent,
who left the stack of papers,
unread for years, yellowing in the old chest,
in the corner of the unused room, unheated,
pastures overgrown, no planting this spring
or next, fields gone fallow, forest taking them back.
Something about the end of things.
How can we say we were misinformed?

A PLACE, A DIRECTION

OLD COUNTRY

Once I lived in a town
with a castle, a famous regiment,
a cathedral. Harvest was golden
with armies of wheat, then came the chill,
day after gray day of rain, fading light.

I cook breakfast and dinner for fifty people
every day, Sunday evening off.
Afternoons I lie in bed to stay warm,
reading Thomas Hardy, then Henry James,
novel follows novel,
like courses in an ever richer meal,
I discover Penguin paperbacks, Colette
and poets, the music of French on one page,
Dans ton île ô Vénus, English facing
like an accusation *on your island Venus*,
No car or stereo,
no television or telephone, a single room,
bed, table, chair, suitcase of clothes,
Do I know that I am poor?
Library card, journal, aerogrammes.

On Wednesday and Sunday the bell ringers
enter the cathedral tower. No matter the weather
I go out to catch the first sound, a cascade
of breaking things, tumbling over each other
making the air new, sharp. Is the field of gravity changing?

I am in a far country, my life is dust,
but these bells, their music
throw a wild glamour over my heart.
They call like gold under water,
I reach through something — cold, swift, flowing,
to touch what gathers the light unto itself
with a hand I do not recognize as my own.

ON THE ISLAND OF HYDRA

Easter holidays,
noisy taverna dinners, I share a table
with a young American couple, newlyweds,
we drink retsina, they buy.
There is dancing.

The husband disappears. She tells me everything.
Her face begins to work, I say, *Let's walk.*
On the dark path beyond the town
where the sea makes itself heard,
we come upon them. They do not hear
or see us. How can they?

I did not know two people
could gleam so in such dark,
a moment becalmed, luminous
like the sudden glow of phosphor
on a moonless sea.

CINQUE TERRE: IN THE VILLAGE
OF MONTALE, THE BAR FEGINA

Each morning walking down from the laureate's villa,
having been wakened by the blasted nightingales,
I turn to the Bar Fegina,
its plate glass windows are open to the sea,
the tired woman behind the bar smiles her Manet smile
and gives me what I want. I do not speak the language.
Beyond the usual politenesses, I have many nouns,
numbers in the hundreds of thousands, no verbs.
It is enough to watch. I spend hours here,
at different times of the day:
early morning is a *caffé latte* with a double espresso,
noonish, before lunch, never lunch here, an aperitif,
at afternoon's end, between five and six,
I sit with a Chanel pink Campari and orange
and regard the shops, the chatter,
small discriminations among the fruit, the lettuces.
The sea is flat at this hour, the sun pyrrhic.
I return at nine or thereafter,
the oven fire is glowing, pizza and fish bake,
the little kitchen steams.
My companions — I let the talk go,
words bursting and subsiding
like froth at wave's end,
we've a carafe of cheap local red
or the fizzy white, very cold.
The sea is black, horizon lighter,
the voice of the sea is constant, unurgent
and for a few hours in the Bar Fegina,
in the village of Monterosso al Mare,
on the Ligurian coast between Portofino and La Spezia,
I have the illusion of being somewhere.

THE DAUGHTER OF THE HOUSE
COMES OF AGE

— Florence, 1480

The world of women is one cloth,
woof and warp, needle and thread,
wheel and shuttle, rooms
farthest from the street,
kitchens, herbs, storerooms,
drawn meat, the wealth of spice,
childbed, the murmurous voices,
their dovelike flutter over the prayers of priests,
the words of poets, their paradise of love,
as familiar in the catalogue of her days
as which servant has tender hands,
the birdseller's delicate cages,
figs sweet with the sun.

There is the maze of a suitor's desires.
Her dreams, a dark forest,
the hunted white hart,
running, hiding,
only to be brought to earth
by the dogs of carnality.

Say *yes*
and everything seems so simple.

The hard fate of the woman who refuses,
la bella inimica.
In Dante's stony rime
six words are repeated like blows:
woman, grass, green, stone, hill, shade,
or is it *shadow*?

Her heart is stone to him, he says.

Her eyes look beyond
to green grass,
vivid black in the hill's shade,
she cannot break stone.
But fire, she burns.

THE DRESS

This dress frightens me,
    impels men I hardly know
        to approach, to say, with a kind of shy,
            halting politeness,
                I like your dress.

Was it Mohammed who said,
    Silk permits the body a second
            nakedness?

Two pieces of silk sewn together falling
    slightly off the shoulder: a simple sheath,
        sleeveless, Greek, archaic,
            some Lapith girl the centaur steals
                from the marriage feast —

water brought up
    from the deep dark well, cold,
        clear as the first moment light takes it,
        how it slakes thirst,
            becomes memory of all water.

HUNTING EARLY

You live in the country of hard-bit words
chokeberry silence,
you caress the dog's silk ear
and hunt in the sweet gun-grease smell of dawn.
All that coffee before first light —
you can piss anywhere.

You fill the bag with bird.
Sun breaks overhead,
you share your biscuit with the dog.
Tired, dew-wet, coat thick with burrs,
she follows you into tree shadow.
Mockers and warblers turn loose the air,
that long walk back is nothing.
It will be hours before memory devours your heart.

AS HEARD EARLY MORNING ON NATIONAL PUBLIC RADIO, SEPTEMBER 16, 1996 WHILE DRIVING FROM ATHENS TO KNOXVILLE

The Coast Guard picked up a woman
three miles off the Florida coast,
not a boat in sight,
she was swimming, strongly, steadily
away from shore, farther into the open sea.
They asked her why she was swimming,
where she was going and she answered
that she was tired of life on earth, and she was
transitioning to her life in the sea.
They took her back to land, to dryness,
to psychiatric examination,
indirect lighting and questions.
How do you feel in traffic
when someone cuts in front of you?
Have you ever hurt a small animal?
She answers but she does not tell
that when she is in the water,
never only water,
but an inverted universe
aswim with the great uncaught, the thronging numbers,
their being the fluid medium, the lighted and star dark sky,
swimming, the whole world swimming,
riding the ribboning currents, and she,
not born of air nor of water,
she is swimming where the light bends.

THE SEMESTER FORREST LIVED IN KENTUCKY

At twilight I drive out of Harlan County, Highway 221,
snake of a road taking up good bottom in a valley so narrow,
not a hundred yards across, bramble, slag, trash, trailers now
with a cover of blackberry blossom thick and wild with white,
overrunning, impossible to contain.

At twilight a woman walks her garden's dark tilth, closely,
closely she regards soft green shoots,
corn, tomatoes, and beans of August, summer of this coming winter.

At twilight a man shoots a basketball through a netless hoop,
that thumping, ringing thud on metal, on backboard,
his arms still out there in their longing reach,
lost to me when I round the bend.

At twilight two blond white-pale children play in a trailer, doorless,
open to whatever wants to come in.

At twilight a man crosses the road to feed what is in the pen.

At twilight the little baby Jesus churches lie still, parking lots full;
along this road crosses say, *Jesus is coming soon,*
and how soon I come upon the woman dressed in white, walking,
her silver-white hair so neatly up, she carries a white plastic bag,
her feet delicate as deer on the narrow shoulder.

At twilight coal trucks take their Sabbath rest,
hydraulic beds point toward heaven, tomorrow
the Bledsoe Coal Corporation will fill its chutes, same iron gray
as sorrow, as coal pulver lying along the road, covering
all who pass, who bear it away, a life digging, black diamonds falling,
tumbling downward of their weight to lightless heaps.

At twilight a woman watches from her porch,
in her lone lifting hand, the knowledge I have passed.

HOW I TURNED UP DEAD
IN THE GROCERY STORE PARKING LOT

At the Food Lion today I am loading groceries
into the car when I notice this old guy,
tall, smoker thin, bleached out blue jeans, faded work shirt
not tucked in, white crew cut, white jaw stubble,
eyes bluer, paler than his jeans. He is pushing
a grocery cart, loaf of white bread,
case of beer, natural, lite,
across the parking lot. He doubles back, weaves
between, around cars, up one row, down another.
I realize, he can't find his car. Ted, 70-something
sacker, comes out to gather stray carts, I almost say something,
but wait, watching the old guy steering his beer and bread
past the same cars he's been by, two, three times now, looking,
not anxious, just focused on his search,
when at last, on the far side of the lot, a car, mud swiped,
windshield grimed, windows rolled down,
sitting by itself pulls his cart like a magnet;
his face shows nothing but the still searching look, no joy, no relief,
he puts the beer in, throws the bread on top, leaving the cart
to its fate in the through lane, he pulls away and I wonder
if he will still be driving tonight, riding down familiar streets,
looking for something he can't quite remember
but knows he is supposed to know, like a voice, like mother's kitchen,
like the way first light comes into the room.
And who am I to talk, who searches dreams and stars for meaning?

58

WHAT'S LEFT WHEN IT WON'T GO AWAY

The butcher at the Bargain Barn
has taken a fancy to me
as I inspect the meat
lying in its fresh red pools,
shining in its cellowrap.
Usually I go for the dead baby-like chicken,
the skinned, boneless, non-analogous breasts,
pulpy pale, plump with hormones
and other chemical desiderata,
it is best not to know
just as I have no desire to know
the butcher, so quick to fling aside
his bloody hand-stained
white cotton apron that by the time
I have finished my shopping,
he is lounging among the check-out girls
with his butcher banter,
and I look at the check I have to write,
my hand making numbers and letters,
sense beyond the store's plate glass windows
the large lighted world
like a flaring thing over all our lives:
the night ahead, each of us going
to apartment, to trailer, to house, to single room,
where waits the source of heat, of love,
that will transform the frozen, the raw,
the left-over and the cold,
into a kind word, a shared look,
into what will feed us all.

CARNY

Once a year, late August,
the odd domes of trailers blossom
like fungi on the fairgrounds.
Night makes everyone equal,
rootless geeks,
slicked up townies, hicks
with their red faces, bright eyes
moon-drawn like moths
to this field adance in blinking electric light,
loudspeakers blaring, smell
of cheap sausages sizzling in their fat,
cotton candy's diaphanous spinning,
apples glowing ruby red, poisonous
from the stepmother's hand.
The wanderer with his sun-hard skin
calls the boys and girls
to the roundabout, the tiltawhirl,
the bullet, the Ferris wheel;
little ones scream in the spook house,
while big boys and men
seek the hungry heart of the hot tent
for strange flesh, the heavy make-up,
eyes older than theft,
cold shivery nipples,
this night's work.
Then Sunday, the field
asking after itself in silence.

WORK, FOR THE NIGHT IS COMING

Your hands smell of the barn,
hateful, how it won't wash off —
it's on you at school,
when you want to touch her.

You can't wait to leave the homeplace,
the fields you wish in hell,
your rage at Father's terror,
how one storm can change everything.
Mother looks at you, the strangeness of
what you look for in books, she will never understand.
Is she forgiven? They die year by year,
that crowd, the kin. Not much to say,
you, the one who with all the words,
go to university, buildings ordered, Greek,
lawns idle with grass, polite flowers,
that first restaurant where you pay at the table.

You never look back,
learn how to talk to town girls
with their soft sweaters,
their lifetime of running water, of indoor toilets.

There are moments now, in the library,
you look back in wonder: the sound marriage,
the books with your name on them,
your children in their professions. You had been so sure.

Library light, how rich it is, gold and heavy with motes,
one clear path to the sky, impossible blue,
still big with the longing you threw there.

You think about her.
How quiet it was in the barn that afternoon,

the light like butter, thick and yellow through the chinks,
what she let you do, how she took you where you wanted to go,
the smell of it, fat with promise, the wine made good.

MORNING COFFEE

It is like when the cafeteria lady, Melinda,
the same one you buy coffee from every morning,
tells you when you ask about the drink station guy,
his name you don't know, but you know
he hasn't been around for a few days,
Melinda tells you his name is Sidney,
his Gloria, the love of his life,
she passed, a stroke, only 48, two kids.
Sidney's? *No, some guy's,* she says.
And you can see it,
not all of it, but enough —
the mother, not so young,
the struggle with work, school, the fear,
not at the end of the month, but two weeks
after payday and it's all gone,
plenty of rice and grits, you know that much,
but it's the things that can't be planned for,
the broken glasses, field trip, flat tire —
and here comes Sidney, it's love, life is good.

The next week he still isn't here.
I ask about him and Melinda says
he was supposed to come in this morning,
but hasn't called. I say it's hard. Melinda says, *Yeah,*
her hand shaking a little, *I buried a baby.*
What do you say to that?
We give each other the look. You know the one.
Even the idea, that kind of loss, is a secret, a threat,
the way an unwanted hand moves over you,
way too sure. I hedge, maybe it didn't happen,
maybe it won't. She's punching numbers
on a cash machine that makes quick gulps
of electronic sound. *I am sorry,* I say.
I know, she says, handing me change.

THE FIFTH IN THIS TIME,
THIS PLACE, THIS WORLD

We were in the country —
do you know what that was,
in those days?
White clapboard, no air conditioning, no television,
a well in back, stone cover, bucket on the ledge,
henyard, outdoor toilet, raw wood and tarpaper,
earthen smell, always damp,
bucket of scraps by the backdoor for chickens and hogs,
two front doors along a porch, swings, rockers, slat-back chairs,
front yard trees, big oaks, a showy maple dense with green,
on three sides fields high with corn.

Was it a funeral? Sunday time, long, long hours
adult talk, no one my age, only little kids.
I go lie down in the Ford's front seat,
turn on the radio, perfectly clear all the way from New York City
a big name, heavy with Russia,
Shostakovitch.
The announcer says The Fifth,
that's all and it begins, I recognize it, not the music
but the feeling.
Daddy and I watch Walter Cronkite, *The Twentieth Century*
every Sunday,
on my lap the *Life Magazine Book of World War II*,
that Uncle Jimmy and Gang-Gang saved pennies for
while Daddy was in the South Pacific,
siege of Leningrad, battle of Stalingrad,
thick, thick layers of coats, bodies, the cold
and Daddy telling me it was the Russian winter
that beat Napoleon, then beat Hitler.
But for me it is this music,
how it makes me cry,
as I lie on the front seat,

looking up at green leaves, and me not ten,
this twentieth century just half over
and maybe it isn't the worst yet,
these big trees knocked down by tanks,
this little house in the country outside Rickman, Tennessee
burning, cattle shot, these bodies, all my family,
no one to bury them, the convoy moves on,
faces turned east, certain, to the inconceivable.

YOU'RE NOT FROM AROUND HERE
November, Highway 127,
Sequatchie Valley, Tennessee

They've stopped along the road
at the place marked Scenic View, three families,
out-of-state tags. Before them is the valley,
long and narrow sweep of it
up to the Cumberland plateau, a raw shelf,
rock and timber standing over a quilt
of field, wood, pasture,
the river you know by its apology of trees.
There are farmhouses,
barns, silos clean as Legos,
cattle still as statues. It's either
bad genre painting or the real thing
where people sweat, stink, and chew,
where bass boats, Dodge Rams, the home-grown
cash crop are the engines of desire.
Closest whiskey is Chattanooga,
Atlanta for abortions, but plenty of beer
at the Golden Gallon, Mr. Zip, or Stop 'n' Go,
the kids all go to Hardee's, McDonald's
but for the locals, WinBob's or the Dunlap Restaurant,
Private Meeting Room, Air Conditioned,
gospel preacher, his Bible-stained voice
caterwauling over the piped in radio,
the sound salty as redeye gravy
over country ham and biscuits,
grits and hash browns,
make those eggs over easy, ma'am,
the regulars are there, best coffee around
but the truckers all know where that trailer is.
Up the hollow, the little lab, dirty and efficient,
turns out the crank that jump-starts your heart,

makes you go faster and faster,
your thoughts like bees in a box,
furious buzzing keeping you on the road,
inside the radio, the cab, the world as long as you're driving,
thinking you just as soon as you can think it.

WHY I LIVE IN THE SOUTH

Git there the fustest with the mostest Forrest said,
I named my first-born Forrest, not for the movie
but the slave-dealer, a general of the South,
of two great-grandfathers, a great killer:
in the name, the burden.
How the stink of history inheres in the soil, the very air —
Vicksburg in August, Holiday Inn, family vacation,
smothering heat, droning air conditioner no respite,
like a bad refrigerator barely keeping the beer cold;
my husband falls asleep faster than the children.
Dark, their breathing, I am hyped, stunned,
waiting for dawn. I am running
in the national cemetery that reeks of magnolia,
packed with marble monuments to Union dead,
why did they build that stuff down here?
All earnest, moral, and upright, didn't they know?
Jesus shoot me — white marble in the South,
Roman allusion, funerary memory, the promise,
the fallen nature of us, everywhere the contradiction
between that past and desire, a contradiction that includes myself,
in love with impossibility, living in a marriage gone beserk,
being held together, at least for this August,
by the road I drive, kids in the back seat
with their Sonic limeades and crayons,
the Lincoln's air-co turned up full blast,
my husband sweating as he sleeps in the front seat,
U.S. Highway 61 to Natchez,
to New Orleans where our past lies
in the heat-softened streets of the Quarter.
When you got the Lincoln, when you got the credit cards
that buy you out of towns where nobody wants to stop,
speed limit twenty-five, cruiser waiting,
names you can't even pronounce
much less believe, Nitta Yuma, Panther Burn, Itta Bena —

they're just places in the rearview mirror.
If you are born there
and you don't own the big house,
like a junk yard dog
you are forever chained to that feral beauty,
one road in, one road out.

GO UP TO COME DOWN, DANCE FOR NOW

— Balanchine

When I am fourteen, I read your story, Amelia Earhart,
I do not wonder why you fly over continents,
oceans, a criss-cross of journeys, point to point,
honor to honor. What house can hold you?
You have sailor's eyes, I think you beautiful,
free as the clouds you roam in.
I go with you, fueled by the desire to escape
from suburban boxes, man, wife, child,
repeated in rows along roads that meet and go on,
punctuated by signs —
stop, careful children, dead end.

I read your story as I lie
across the bed in my sky-blue room,
my head pillowed in the window,
while overhead airport traffic
slices morning and afternoon
into takeoff and landing,
the ecstatic going up to come down.
Those shining silver planes —
how the heavy propeller drone
like an echo of some deep earth-torn throb
gives way to the jet, its high, excited scream.
I grow up, marry, have children of my own,
Amelia Earhart, I disappear with you in the Pacific of our sex.

READING *PATRIOTIC GORE*

For Jan on the eve of her surgery

Reading Bertram Wyatt-Brown's review of a Southern history
took me to a dusty bookshelf, Wilson's paperback bought
for some long forgotten class, in search of
those Southern well-born women, wartime downfall.
Richard Wright said Southern women are ghosts —
all I know is one family's experience, partial,
a glimpse into a past lost, fragmented,
distorted by successive mirrors from down the hall,
an enfilade of possibilities, ending in me,
writing this, one more attempt, one more failure.

The oblivion of a mass grave at Shiloh — he was just a cousin,
John Jefferson Neathery, died April 6, 1862, without issue,
and another of my endless corridor of cousins, Cheryl,
teaches history in the public schools of Franklin, Tennessee,
not so no one will forget but that someone will remember something,
a scent, a fabric's coarse rasp on the skin, the sound of a voice.

And now Cheryl's two, Courtney and Chase,
with their country club names, Williamson County's finest,
baseball and ballet, Barbie and soccer, how do we tell them?
What was it like — no easier, no harder than making sense of
what Buck Preston is telling, her head lolling
on Mary Chestnutt's knee, Mary slowly stroking that dark red hair,
the fire crackling and tumbling into ash in the large bare room,
Buck's voice, going on and on in those soft tidewater slurs,
the inexorable story that sex must triumph over death,
ingallant, ludicrous, unlovely, and unsafe,
that a man's sudden, overwhelming embrace
has a greater consequence than the fall of Richmond,
for after all, that will happen anyway.

YEAH, SURE

I'm drinking a longneck in the backseat,
car door open
to afternoon heat, Natchez,
my hair is long, lank with sweat,
a family vacation,
station wagon broke down in Memphis,
but a rental came through, so
here I am with him, the kids, Mississippi in August,
their necks ringed with grime, hands sticky,
each night, a different motel, they come out of the bath
smelling sweetly, ready for their story. He and I take turns.

Our white Lincoln is parked on this bluff to catch a breeze,
we look up and down the river
like we are going to see some rescuing hand
come right down from heaven to straighten us up
or at least put us in a movie with a happy ending.
He doesn't know it yet, his mind twisting,
turning on itself, but he's getting rid of me.
I'm wearing a white teeshirt, a red silk skirt limp and hot,
no ideas, but scared and happy, dreaming poems,
who's stealing my sugar? Two mornings later
that Lincoln crosses Lake Pontchartrain
to New Orleans where maybe things will be different.
I mail the letter anyway. Just in case.

LYRICS

ATTAR

The beauty of life flares out at us
from the cracks and fissures
of the broken road we walk
without looking, without hearing,
heeding some inner call that is distraction,
but in the wanting we forget, no,
we do not remember to look, to hear until we trip,
and in falling, the instinctive thrust of hands
to catch ourselves, in falling, suddenly
how beautiful, layer upon layer of bird call,
that distant train's melancholy horn, who knew
tulips in such colors, the black purple of a dead king's heart?

～

What is the secret
coiled in the hearts of roses?
Breathe, they say, this scent
that breaks your heart,
that you will confound in memory,
with memory, no forgetting there,
these thorns you remember
in your care, in how you hold me
as your face turns to your desire.

～

Rose
brief,
brief in its beauty
but the scent
better than fame.

～

What can one do,
when one has survived love?
I am like that city
shaken to rubble
by quaking earth,
burnt and scattered
by war's swift rage —
now grass grows
in bursts of sudden green,
rainwater gathers new blue,
a flower's wild return
is announced through broken things.

∽

In the nightbreath,
in the longing for home the dark brings,
in the quick-beating hearts of birds,
voices silent at last, when the sleeping world leans in
to the near audible hum of insect, to the quiet rustle
in the brief rise and fall of leaf and branch,
to the near motionless current of air,
rising and falling as breath releases body
from thought to memory, from memory to dream —
so we journey through this night's dark mirror,
the wrong true thing we walk into, gladly.

∽

And Helen returns

Sweet the cheat
to eke out
wind-whipped winters,
thrift of vengeance,
arid summers,
flat light, sheep stink,
spring, swift sharp sting,
dream and memory —
night's twin thieves.

WHY I DRINK

Those lying myths have it
when rosy fleshed Amphelos
was killed by that bull,
Dionysus wept.

His tears water the ground
where Amphelos lies.
The twining vine of love
that binds two hearts
becomes the vine heavy
with clusters of rosy fruit.

Dionysus takes the fruit,
crushes it in his hands,
grapesweet, empurpled
like the blood of roses,
the juice stains hands, lips.

He tastes first the wine of memory,
then the elixir of forgetting.

HIGH SUMMER, HOME FROM WORK

I am drinking the first martini,
eating Danish blue cheese with saltines
and there are olives from Italy,
oil cured in their tight
little mummy bodies.
My air-cooled house is a pleasure,
private, hermetic,
against heat, against light,
just this concentrate of Mediterranean
in the mouth, ginever, herbs,
and the dizz at the back of the head
that flowers down the junctures
through the tired body till the day,
the hour, the burr of blue cheese blending
with martini bite, all seem to slur into well-being.
Have you heard this story before?

SAPIENS

While we live,
some atavistic hominid
always exists,
with not much of a thumb,
a disposition, a tending
toward earth,
insect-loving, always hungry,
so many teeth,
joy of chewing,
that jaw like a hinge
to this low, low brow,
memory in every part of the mouth.

WHAT PINDAR MEANS
BY *THE SWEET WRONG THING*

For my birthday
I drank a bottle of champagne
alone.
I can do this
which is why
I have so few poems,
if not birthdays.

It was Eros
who gave me the cup,
Eros, who brought
that wine to my mouth,
but the thirst,
that was mine.

We all come
to the end we seek,
ruin and death push close,
closer,
crowding time,
the reckoning joined.

ENDINGS

A KEY TO ENDINGS

from a lecture given by Donald Justice
at the Sewanee Writers' Conference — July 22, 1998

They are terminal signs, endings,
expectations of nothing further,
a place in the road, no going past.
Nothing is solved.

There is the marriage or death of the hero.
Not to mention the heroine.

Is lyric a commonplace,
sharp drawing, soft feeling?

There must be more
than a wish to be expressive.

Just the facts,
perhaps an observation of the weather,
the scenery.

Quests or journeys may begin with endings.

When does action become meaning?
Both may be avoided.

As for natural events,
why do we think meaning inheres?
Because it does.
Certain emotions are surely called forth
by geography, the weather of the heart.

And the pure ending?
This is when the sentence realizes itself.

Remember when they distributed the prizes?

Wholeness, harmony, radiance:
of these three I wish to speak of radiance.

At the end of things
we are given one side of the equation,
the other unstated.
And it satisfies,
all essence, of a radiance compact.

All beauty is local.

OUT OF THESE THINGS

The housewives of Hartford in their clapboard houses
watch the poet walk to work.
He is composing to the measure of his step,
to leaf mass overhead, its tremblant green, suburban *luxe*,
those shrubberies, children's hiding places, paths,
houses built for safe-keeping
each room, its light, its heft of air.

In her inmost interior of beige
the housewife fingers the page:
from whom must she steal this moment?
She reads the poet who puts her body in a book,
who draws her breath into the word,
into the fall and tumble of words
she breaks her voice upon, heart coming after.

ETYMOLOGY

Solace that sweet word
is from the Latin *solacium*,
meaning comfort, especially in grief,
calamity, destruction —
the verb is transitive: I console,
you allay. He, she, it assuages.
We soothe.

Beware of those who cannot soothe
themselves: they do damage.

John Donne prayed for God
to shower his graces
upon our peregrination here.
Peregrination calls upon an old,
by now obsolete, meaning — a stay
in a foreign country. Sojourn or exile?

Why resist narrative? *Here*, this land
of currency, language, mother,
implies *there*, unnamed, unlocated place.

I wander and I sleep in the same bed
each night. Melville wrote a poem
on the death of Hawthorne. 'Monody,'
he called it, one voice, echo and lament —
loved him, to have loved him
after loneness long —
words are his solace. He pleads,
ease me a little ease
my song.

How we cling to meaning,
one handheld certainty to the next,
how we love our sweet fictions,
most desirable in the moment of turning away.

WHERE DOES *TERROR* COME FROM?

Terrible is not the same as awful,
atheos, parent to our atheist,
does not mean disbeliever
but abandoned by the gods.
The algorithmic revolution,
relentless, ongoing, apparently
permanent, felt if not heard,
makes people nervous, fearful.
They cling even more tightly
to the most primitive impulses,
like fastening prayers on the head
of a god with no ears,
throwing flowers in a grave
or standing under the marriage canopy,
promising, promising.

A WORD FROM HEANEY'S TRANSLATION OF *BEOWULF*

Hurt-in-hiding
sounds like the name of a flower,
white at the petals' tips,
almost transparent,
like blue thin milk,
a white that deepens to a thick cream
which somehow,
as only flowers can,
bruises to a rich Italian night sky,
above Urbino, say.
The petals are few;
they droop,
sad as sex,
on a long green stalk,
out-braved by the bolder,
bee seducing,
sun hungry thrusters.

FOR JACK

Write a poem about that,
he says as he opens an umbrella
and puts it on top of the table.
You know the kind, collapsible,
black nylon, cheap,
sold in supermarkets,
drugstores, airports
from those racks by the door,
convenient,
when rain surprises you,
when you have no lover.

MEMORIAL DAY

A three egg omelette for lunch
with cheese, a Diet Coke, slice of lemon,
awful sop to the god of thin, later
I shall run — all that heart business,
anti-aging, but I am already thinking about
how much I can drink tonight and still read
with attention Livy's history of Rome.
Maytime, this nation is at war
in some sad old country, frontiers of pink, blue,
and yellow. Oak hydrangea scent the air,
linens dry in sun, the dove of afternoon mourn,
a lawn mower whines several blocks away.
How we fat ourselves on noise, confuse
not remembering with forgetting.
Livy said, *the study of history is the best medicine
for a sick mind* — before empire, envy, ambition,
that Rome stands, an austere building, uncluttered,
clean with hard work. Livy translates Rome's lexis of fit,
the keystone placed *so* permits the arch,
engineers of syntax construct the roads
straight to the great urban heart where bronze heads,
eyeless, watch time gather, wheel, and disperse,
the swallows at twilight in their empire of air.

TEARS ARE NOT ARGUMENTS

— Machado de Assis

The week you died
cherries were coming in.
Bruising the cherries,
I put them in sweet vermouth,
Canadian whiskey to make a Manhattan
the week you died,
not for you that cold of north and ice,
I add more ice to the whiskey
before bruising the cherries,
high summer, star jasmine, honeysuckle —
the early mornings we ran, remember?
The week you died, the missed call, the letter
that will never arrive, I do remember
when bruising the cherries, cutting with the delicate knife,
I watch how they bleed into the drink,
and eat a few, staining my lips red,
while bruising the cherries
for that sweet and bitter drink
the week you died.

NEMESIS

Nemesis is what cannot be undone,
does not mean the meal burning
while voices topple over each other in rage, that slap,
or the slow ooze of blood in the locked house,
or that second the car leaves the road
and you see the person next to you
for the last time.
Nemesis is payback, the whole deal,
what is due for what you thought was over,
let's call it a redistribution,
a consequence
we don't see coming,
a place where there is no rewind, no delete,
the ending
we cannot take back by telling another story,
another *once upon a time*,
always about to be, voice emerging
out of the dark, into the silence
where the secret thing waits,
this daughter of night who never sleeps.

GIRL

Give me your hand as though
you were a child entering,
passing through strange rooms
lived in by relatives you don't know.
They know you
from the day you were born,
and your parents before.
You will remember these rooms,
familiar as the smell of clean cotton
dried on a clothesline,
mystery of the medicine cabinet,
camphophenique bottle
green as a beetle, dusty roses talcum powder.
By the basin lavender soap
makes soft and sweet the sad old flesh.
In this house the hours are
neatly laid out on the dressing table,
nothing touching, rows precise,
brushes, combs, silver-backed mirror,
fruitwood glove box like a reliquary
among bottles of perfume, alluring as liqueurs
too fine to open, scent enough for this past
already present, already lost,
although you have touched as many things as possible,
and broken nothing,
before you've even asked for anything to eat.

TO THE MOON —

An Den Mond

Autumn again, Schubert on the radio —
a language I do not know
yet a tone, quiet despair singing to the moon
out of stillness and night,
makes something real on this American street
almost two centuries away
where moonlight, color of old wedding dresses
darkens earth, deepens shadows. O deathless love:
I believed, a child of suburbia, what was between them,
mystery of adults, what the dark held —
trees at summer's end breathe their emanations over me
as I climb on the back of Eddie Sandlin's motorcycle,
we ride through that night; our loud throb
takes the place of thought.
So much I do not know but that excitement — speed —
silk whipping the face, his body flattened against mine,
both of us moving into the machine —
dark song, by what road,
by what lostness, have I learned of endings?

ABOUT THE AUTHOR

Patricia Waters was born and reared in Nashville, Tennessee. She took her B.A. in history and English at what is now the University of Memphis. After completing several seasons in field archaelogy in Europe, she returned to complete her M.A. in English at the University of Tennessee, Knoxville. She was a teacher, journalist, and community activist in Memphis and New Orleans. She returned to Livingston, Tennessee to rear her children, and later moved to Athens. While teaching at Tennessee Wesleyan College, a generous faculty grant, funded by the Pew Foundation, sent her to writers' conferences — in particular the Sewanee Writers' Conference. Long association with the master teachers at Sewanee, particularly Howard Nemerov, Anthony Hecht, and Donald Justice were crucial to her development as a poet. She returned to UTK to complete her doctorate in English in 1998. After completing a post-doc year in the College of Education, she was writer-in-residence at the University of Tennessee libraries in 2003-2004. She lives in Athens, Tennessee.